LIVING ON A BUDGET

SALE!
Today
Only

CECILIA MINDEN

Published in the United States of America by Cherry Lake Publishing
Ann Arbor, Michigan
www.cherrylakepublishing.com

Math Education: Dr. Timothy Whiteford, Associate Professor of Education at St. Michael's College
Financial Adviser: Kenneth Klooster, financial adviser at Edward Jones Investments
Reading Adviser: Marla Conn, ReadAbility, Inc.

Photo Credits: © Digital Vision/Thinkstock Images, cover, 1, 22; © PathDoc/Shutterstock Images, 5; © JNP/
Shutterstock Images, 6; © Mila Supinskaya/Shutterstock Images, 9; © monkeybusinessimages/Thinkstock Images, 10;
© Alxcrs/Shutterstock Images, 13; © Jupiterimages/Shutterstock Images, 15; © Brand X Pictures/Shutterstock Images,
16; © Sergey Novikov, 19; © antoniodiaz/Shutterstock Images, 21; © Melinda Millward, 25; © DragonImages/
Thinkstock Images, 26; © ponsulak/Shutterstock Images, 27; © Robert Kneschke/Shutterstock Images, 29

Library of Congress Cataloging-in-Publication Data

Minden, Cecilia.
    Living on a budget / Cecilia Minden.
    pages cm. — (Real world math: personal finance)
    Includes index.
    ISBN 978-1-63362-572-3 (hardcover) — ISBN 978-1-63362-752-9 (pdf) — ISBN 978-1-63362-662-1 (pbk.) —
    ISBN 978-1-63362-842-7 (ebook) 1. Budgets, Personal—Juvenile literature. 2. Finance, Personal—
Juvenile literature. I. Title.

    HG179.M5254 2015
    332.024—dc23   2014048642

Cherry Lake Publishing would like to acknowledge the work of
the Partnership for 21st Century Skills. Please visit *www.p21.org*
for more information.

Printed in the United States of America
Corporate Graphics

ABOUT THE AUTHOR

Cecilia Minden, PhD, is an educational consultant and author of many books for children. She is
the former director of the Language and Literacy Program at Harvard Graduate School of Education
in Cambridge, Massachusetts.

TABLE OF CONTENTS

CHAPTER 1

WHAT IS A BUDGET?

Has this ever happened to you? On Saturday, you have $20 in your pocket. On the following Tuesday, you're broke. What happened to your money? It's time to learn how to make and follow a budget!

What is a budget? A budget is a plan for how you are going to use your **income** to pay for your **expenses**. Your income is how much money you receive through jobs or gifts. Your expenses are how you spend that income. Your goal is to have a **balanced budget**. A balanced budget means your income is enough to pay

If you don't make a budget, you're more likely to run out of money.

all of your expenses. Balancing your budget is a skill you will need all of your life.

Creating a budget begins with income. An allowance is one type of income. In some families, the amount of your allowance is related to what jobs you do around the house. Wages are another type of income. Wages are earned when you work for others. Gifts are also a source of income. You might receive money for birthdays or other special occasions. Allowances, wages, and gifts are three ways that students can receive income.

If you like buying video games, you'll need to work that into your budget.

LIFE AND CAREER SKILLS

Savings are an important part of your budget. Put your savings in a bank or credit union so your money will earn **interest**. Interest is what the banks pay you to keep your money with them. Let's say you saved $30.00 a month in a savings account earning 5 percent interest. At the end of five years, you would have more than $2,000.00 in your account!

Think about how you spend your money. Do you like to buy snacks or other treats? Do you spend money on computer games or music? Do you buy your own clothing? Your expenses may be all these as well as donations to charity, or buying gifts. And you might put money from your income into your savings account. Keeping a balanced budget isn't hard, but it does take some planning. Let's get started!

REAL WORLD MATH CHALLENGE

Jacob's parents give him $18.00 a week as an allowance. On the days that Jacob doesn't want to bring lunch from home, he has to use his own money to buy lunch at the school cafeteria. Jacob uses $12.00 each week for lunches, donates $2.00 a week to a charity at school, puts $4.00 in savings, and spends $2.50 on snacks.

- What are Jacob's weekly expenses?
- Does he have a balanced budget?

(Turn to page 30 for the answers)

Where Does Your Money Go?

Before you set up a budget, you need to think about how and where you spend your money. The most important question to ask about each item is, do I need it or do I just want it?

Needs are what you must have to survive. The most basic needs are food, water, and shelter. Other needs are what you must have to live your life. These needs will change at different stages in your life.

A student's basic needs are usually taken care of by an adult. Talk to your family about items you are

Even a small donation goes a long way to those in need of help.

expected to buy. These may include clothing, transportation, and school supplies. Not every student has the same needs. For example, you may need to buy sports gear. Another student may need to buy sheet music.

Wants are things you would like to have but don't need to survive. Expensive clothing, concert tickets, and laptops are nice to have but are not a basic need. You can't buy all of your wants, but you can have some of them if you plan carefully. Always make sure your needs are taken care of first when you plan a budget. Then figure out how to pay

Would a cell phone be a want or a need? A cell phone could be a need for emergencies, but the extra apps and games would be a want.

for the wants that are most important to you.

The first step in creating a budget is to figure out your income and expenses. Buy a small notebook to keep in your pocket or purse. Label it "Money Diary." For two weeks, write down every item you buy and how much it costs. At the end of two weeks, you will know exactly how you spent your money. Use this information to create your budget.

REAL WORLD MATH CHALLENGE

Grace wanted to create a budget.
She began by keeping a money diary for two weeks:

Grace's Money Diary for February 1 to February 14

DATE	INCOME	EXPENSE
February 1	$20.00 Allowance	
February 3		$15.00 Clothing
February 4		$2.00 Donation to animal shelter
February 5	$25.00 Birthday	
February 5		$8.00 Movie ticket, $8.00 snacks
February 5		$12.00 School lunch card
February 8	$20.00 Allowance	
February 9		$1.65 Paper and pencils at the school store
February 10	$7.25 Raked leaves	
February 11		$5.43 Souvenir shop at the art museum (field trip)

- What was Grace's income from February 1 to February 14?
- What were Grace's expenses for that time period?
- Which expenses were needs? How much did Grace spend on them?
- Which expenses were wants? How much did Grace spend on them?
- Grace would like to download a new album. Does she have the $13.50 to pay for it?

(Turn to page 30 for the answers)

DO THE MATH: CREATE A SIMPLE BUDGET

Some income and expenses stay the same from week to week. These are called **fixed** income and fixed expenses. For example, a fixed income would be your allowance or wages. Fixed expenses might include school lunches, donations to charity, or **deposits** into a savings account. This is the base for creating your budget.

You also have **variable** income and expenses. Variable means that amounts change from month to month. You might have more income one week

Money for snacks or entertainment may be one of your budget's variable expenses.

because you were given money as a birthday present. You might have more expenses the following week because you had to buy extra supplies for a school project.

Use the budget on page 17 as a guide for creating your budget. Enter your fixed income. You can estimate your variable income. Estimate means you will put in a number close to what you think it will be. For example, if you usually get between $5.00 and $10.00 for babysitting, then maybe put $8.00 in your budget.

Make one column for what you plan to spend and one column for what you actually spent. This helps you keep track of exactly where you spent more than you had budgeted.

Make a list of your fixed and variable expenses and enter them in your budget. Use the sample as a guide to fill out your budget. Think about your short- and long-term goals. Short-term goals are things you want to be able to buy within a few weeks or months. A short-term goal might be a concert ticket, a DVD, or a computer game. Long-term goals, like a car, are things that cost more money and will take many months or even years of saving. Include both of these in your budget.

LIFE AND CAREER SKILLS

Remember to make room in your budget for charitable donations. Setting aside just $1.00 a week is a yearly donation of $52.00.

Your parents need to make a budget for household expenses.

Before you spend money on something, make sure you have enough money left in that category of your budget.

Now comes the fun part! Divide your money, putting an amount in each category on your list. You will need to play around with this for a bit to make it come out even.

In her budget, Grace has planned all her expenses for the next two weeks. She included saving for both short- and long-term goals. Grace wasn't sure if she would be doing any chores for neighbors in the next two weeks, so she left that line blank.

REAL WORLD MATH CHALLENGE

Budget for February 15 to February 28 (2 weeks)

CATEGORY	BUDGETED AMOUNT	ACTUAL AMOUNT	DIFFERENCE
Fixed income allowance			
$40.00 ($20.00 paid on February 15 and February 22)	$40.00		
Variable income			
Chores for neighbors?			
TOTAL	$40.00		
Fixed Expenses			
School lunches	$24.00		
Donation to animal shelter	$2.00		
Short-term goal	$1.00		
Long-term goal	$1.00		
Variable Expenses			
School supplies	$0.75		
Snacks	$1.25		
Entertainment	$10.00		
TOTAL	$40.00		

- What are Grace's total expenses?
- Grace decides she wants to save more for her short- and long-term goals. She changes her budget for entertainment to $7.00 and her budget for snacks to $0.75. She puts the rest in savings, dividing it equally between short- and long-term goals.
- How much does she put in each of these two categories?

(Turn to page 30 for the answers)

Do the Math: Living on a Budget

Have you ever heard somebody say that an idea "looked good on paper"? This means that ideas don't always work out quite the way you had planned. A budget is a plan for how you will spend your money. But once the money is actually in your pocket, you may need to make adjustments to your budget. Why? Life is full of unexpected events. What do you do if the child you babysit every Saturday evening gets so sick that her parents decide to stay home with her? Your income for the week will be lower. You're going to have to adjust your budget to take that into account.

Walking pets is a way to earn extra cash and get some exercise.

Grace stuck to her budget (on page 17) the first week, but it fell apart the second week. On Tuesday, a neighbor asked Grace to do yard work on Saturday. She would earn $20.00 for the job. On Friday, Grace bought a pair of shoes on sale for $19.99. She borrowed the money from her mom, promising to pay her back with her earnings from the yard work. It rained all day Saturday, so Grace lost her job. Grace now has to trim her budget so that she can pay for the unexpected expense. Trimming a budget means reducing expenses.

REAL WORLD MATH CHALLENGE

Updated Budget for February 15 to February 28 (2 weeks)

CATEGORY	BUDGETED AMOUNT	ACTUAL AMOUNT	DIFFERENCE
My new fixed income allowance			
$20.00 per week (paid only on February 15)	$20.00		
My new variable income			
Chores for neighbors	$0.00		
TOTAL	$20.00		
Need to lower my fixed expenses			
School lunches	$24.00		
Donation to animal shelter	$2.00		
Short-term goal	$2.75		
Long-term goal	$2.75		
Need to lower my variable expenses			
School supplies	$0.75		
Snacks	$0.75		
Entertainment	$7.00		
TOTAL	$40.00		

- Grace owes her mom $20.00 for the new shoes. They agree as Grace's way of paying her back, her mom will withhold her allowance on February 22, which would have been $20.00. Now Grace will have to make her allowance from February 15 last until her next one, on March 1.
- Grace looks at her budget. She decides that she will still buy school supplies, but not any snacks. She will make the same deposit for her short-term goal, but nothing for her long-term goal. She will cut in half her school lunches, shelter donation, and entertainment budgets. Will this be enough to make up for the shoes?

(Turn to page 30 for the answers)

Helping a neighbor with a garden is a good way to earn some extra money.

Grace likes doing yard work for neighbors, but it's supposed to rain for the next week. Rather than finding a new job, Grace decides to follow her tighter budget until she pays her mom back. This means it will take longer for her to save enough money to buy that new computer game she wants.

Though making her budget work was hard, Grace learned some good lessons. She learned that she needed to rework her budget to include an emergency fund. She decides to divide up her savings money. She plans to put

If there's something you would buy regularly, paying the sale price is a good way to lower your expenses.

away $2.00 each for short-term and long-term goals and to put $1.50 in a savings account for emergency expenses.

A budget is like a road map. Most maps show you how many miles you have to travel to reach your goal. As you head down the road, however, you might decide to head off toward a place that looks like fun. Taking that detour will keep you from reaching your goal.

The same is true of your budget. A budget is your plan to reach your goal. The more money you spend on things you don't need, the longer it will take you to reach your goal. Always pay for your basic needs first and put money into your savings before you do anything else. The money that remains is yours to spend as you like. Putting money into savings first allows you to take an occasional side trip and still end up at your goal on time.

Once in a while, when you go on a car trip, you'll get a flat tire. Having a spare tire in the trunk is the best way to get back on the road quickly. An emergency savings account is like a spare tire in the trunk. Set aside an amount every month. If you have to use the emergency money, replace it as soon as you can. You want to be ready if another flat tire slows you down!

Tools to Help You Budget

Sticking to a budget takes practice and effort. There are many tools available to you as you learn to create and follow your personal budget.

A quick and cheap way is a notebook, a three-ring binder, a pencil, and a box of envelopes. Use the notebook to keep track of all your expenses just as you did in chapter two. You can keep your budget sheets in the three-ring binder. If you have access to a computer, you could create budget sheets using the sample in chapter three. Make your own changes so your budget really fits your needs.

One way to budget is to put cash in separate envelopes.

Keep your budget book and all of your receipts together. Receipts are tickets showing how much you spent and where. Use one envelope for each of your expense categories. Mark each envelope with the name of the category. Keep separate envelopes for savings, short-term goals, and long-term goals. Paste a picture of the item you are saving for on each envelope. It will remind you of your goal. Put the exact amount of money for each category in each envelope. You will be able to know exactly how much you have to spend.

Many Web sites will help you set up a personal budget.

If you have a computer or smartphone, then you can keep your budget at your fingertips. There are several Web sites suggested on page 31 that can help you set up and maintain a budget. They also offer great tips on how to save your money. Use your computer as you would the notebook, keeping track of all income and expenses.

A smartphone means you are only an app away from a budget you can call up wherever you are. You can instantly record your expenses, check your bank balances, and determine if you are getting the best price for what you want to buy. Before you download an app, however, do your research. Read the reviews to see what others think of the app. Get one that will be easy and quick for you to use, or else you may quit budgeting! Some apps are free and others cost money. And always, check with your parents before buying anything online.

You can keep a running record of your expenses in your phone. Use the notepad feature or download an app designed for this purpose.

As a kid, adults usually pay for your basic needs of food, shelter, and clothing. But when you get older, you will have to pay for all your own expenses with your own income. That's what it means to be financially responsible. By managing a small budget now, you will learn the skills to handle bigger budgets in the future. Businesses, schools, teams, and families all use budgets. So do cities, counties, and countries. Learning how to make a budget and stick to it is a skill you will use your entire life.

21ST CENTURY CONTENT

Walmart is the biggest employer in the United States. Its income was $118 billion in 2014. And in February 2015, it announced it would be raising the pay of about one-third of its workforce, or half a million people. Imagine balancing that budget!

A chief financial officer (CFO) is responsible for financial planning and record keeping of a company.

Real World Math Challenge Answers

CHAPTER ONE
Page 7

Jacob's income totals: $18.00
Jacob's expenses totals: $20.50
The difference is $2.50.

Jacob does not have a balanced budget.
$18.00 is less than $20.50

CHAPTER TWO
Page 11

Grace's income was $72.25.
$20.00 + $25.00 + $7.25 + $20.00 = $72.25

Grace's expenses totaled $64.08.
$15.00 + $2.00 + $8.00 + $8.00 + $12.00 + $1.65 +
$5.43 = $52.08

Grace's needs were her lunch cards and school
supplies. She spent a total of $13.65 on needs.
$12.00 + $1.65 = $13.65

Grace's wants were the clothes, movie, snacks,
donation, and souvenir. She spent a total of
$38.43 on wants.
$15.00 + $8.00 + $8.00 + $2.00 + $5.43 = $38.43

Grace does have enough for the album. She has
$20.17 remaining.
$72.25 − $52.08 = $20.17

CHAPTER THREE
Page 17

In Grace's first budget, her expenses total $40.00.
$24.00 + $2.00 + $1.00 + $1.00 + $0.75 + $1.25 +
$10.00 = $40.00

After lowering her entertainment and snacks budgets,
Grace's expenses total $36.50.
$24.00 + $2.00 + $1.00 + $1.00 + $0.75 + $0.75 +
$7.00 = $36.50
This enables Grace to save an additional $3.50.
$40.00 − $36.50 = $3.50

Grace puts aside an extra $1.75 for short-term goals
and an extra $1.75 for long-term goals, for a total of
$2.75 in each category.
$3.50 ÷ 2 = $1.75
$1.75 + $1.00 = $2.75

CHAPTER FOUR
Page 20

If Grace makes all of those changes, she will have
exactly enough money.

$12.00 + $1.00 + $2.75 + $0.75 + $3.50 = $20.00

FIND OUT MORE

BOOKS

Larson, Jennifer S. *Do I Need? Or Do I Want It? Making Budget Choices*. Minneapolis: Lerner, 2010.

Randolph, Ryan. *How to Make a Budget*. New York: PowerKids Press, 2014.

Wiseman, Blaine. *Budgeting*. New York: Weigl, 2009.

WEB SITES

Hands on Banking: Take Charge of Your Future
www.handsonbanking.org/
This site has an interactive program that teaches banking and money management skills.

Kids.gov: Money
http://kids.usa.gov/money/index.shtml
See links to many government sites with information, games, and videos on money and banking for kids.

PBS: It's My Life
http://pbskids.org/itsmylife/money/managing/article7.html
Find money management information and games at this site.

GLOSSARY

balanced budget (BAL-uhnst BUHJ-it) a plan where you have enough money for everything you need

deposits (dih-PAH-zutz) amounts of money put in a bank

expenses (ik-SPENS-ez) money for a particular job or task

fixed (FIKST) an amount that does not change

income (IN-kuhm) the money that a person earns or receives, especially from working

interest (IN-trist) the amount earned on money kept in a bank

variable (VAHR-ee-uh-bul) subject to change

INDEX